The Story of Creation

In the
BEGINNING

From Genesis, Chapter One
of the Holy Bible

CROSSWAY BOOKS · WHEATON, ILLINOIS

A Division of Good News Publishers

IN THE BEGINNING

Copyright ©1998 by Good News Publishers

Published by Crossway Books
a division of Good News Publishers
1300 Crescent Street
Wheaton, Illinois 60187

Concept and design: D² Designworks
Photography: ©Tony Stone Images

ISBN 0-89107-997-1
First printing, 1998
Printed in Singapore

Bible quotations are taken from the *King James Version* of the Holy Bible.

LIBRARY OF CONGRESS CATALOGING-IN-PUBLICATION DATA

In the beginning : the story of creation.
    p. cm.
    Summary : Presents the story of God's creation of the world as described
in the book of Genesis, illustrated with photographs.
    ISBN 0-89107-997-1 (hc : alk. paper)
    1. Bible stories, English—O.T. Genesis. 2. Creation—Biblical teaching—
Juvenile literature. [1. Creation. 2. Bible stories—O.T.] I. Crossway Books.
BS651. I56 1998
222'.1109505—dc21   97-45994
                                                           CIP
                                                           AC

07   06   05   04   03   02   01   00   99   98
15 14 13 12 11 10 9 8 7 6 5 4 3 2 1

Does the eagle soar at your command and build his nest on high? Do you send the lightning

bolts on their way? Have you comprehended the vast expanses of the earth? Where were you

when I laid the earth's foun-  dation? Tell me, if you under-

stand. Who marked off its dimensions? Surely you know!

Who stretched a measuring line across it? On what were its footings set, or who laid its

cornerstone— while the morning stars sang together and all the angels shouted for joy?

In the beginning God created the heavens and the earth.

And the earth was without form,

and void;

and darkness was upon the face of the deep.

And the Spirit of God moved upon the face of the waters.

And God said, Let there be light.

And there was light.

God saw the light, that it was good.

And God divided the light

from the darkness.

God called the light Day,

and the darkness he called Night.

And the evening and the morning

were the first day.

And God said, Let there be a

firmament in the midst of the waters,

and let it divide the waters from the waters.

And God made the firmament,

and divided the waters which were

under the firmament

from the waters which were above the firmament.

And it was so.

And God called the firmament Heaven.

And the evening and the morning

were the second day.

And God said,

Let the waters under the heaven
be gathered together unto one place,
and let the dry land appear.

And it was so.

And God called the dry land Earth;

and the gathering together of the waters he called Seas. And God saw that it was good.

And God said, Let the earth bring forth grass,

and the herb yielding seed, and the fruit tree yielding fruit after its kind,

whose seed is in itself, upon the earth. And it was so.

And the earth brought forth grass,

and herbs yielding seed after their kind,

and the tree yielding fruit,

whose seed was in itself, after its kind.

And God saw that it was good.

And the evening and the morning were the third day.

And God said,

Let there be lights in the firmament of the heaven

to divide the day from the night;

and let them be for signs, and for seasons,

and for days, and years.

And let them be for lights in the firmament

of the heaven to give light upon the earth.

And it was so.

And God made two great lights:

the greater light to rule the day,

and the lesser light to rule the night;

He made the stars also.

And God set them in the firmament of the heaven

to give light upon the earth,

and to rule over the day

and over the night,

and to divide the light from the darkness.

And God saw that it was good.

And the evening and the morning

were the fourth day.

And God said, Let the waters bring forth

abundantly moving creatures that have life,

and birds that may fly above the earth

in the open firmament of heaven.

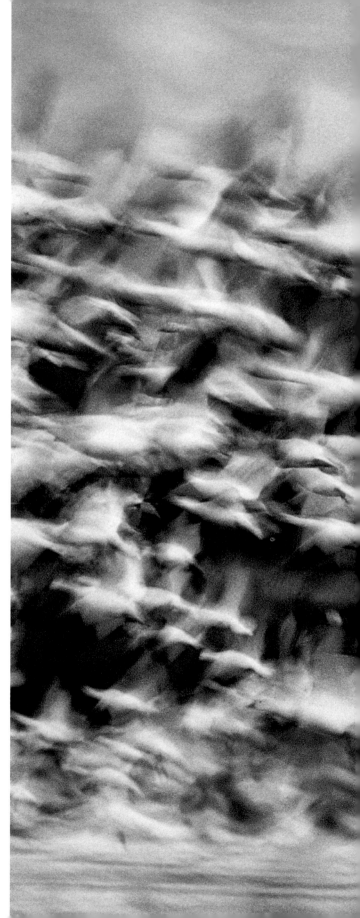

And God created great fish,

  and every living creature that moves

which the waters brought forth abundantly,

after their kind,

and every winged bird after its kind.

And God saw that it was good.

And God blessed them, saying,

Be fruitful, and multiply,

and fill the waters in the seas,

and let birds multiply in the earth. And the

evening and the morning were the fifth day.

And God said,

Let the earth bring forth the living creatures

after their kind,

cattle, and creeping things,

and beasts of the earth after their kind.

And it was so.

And God made the beasts of the earth

after their kind, and cattle after their kind,

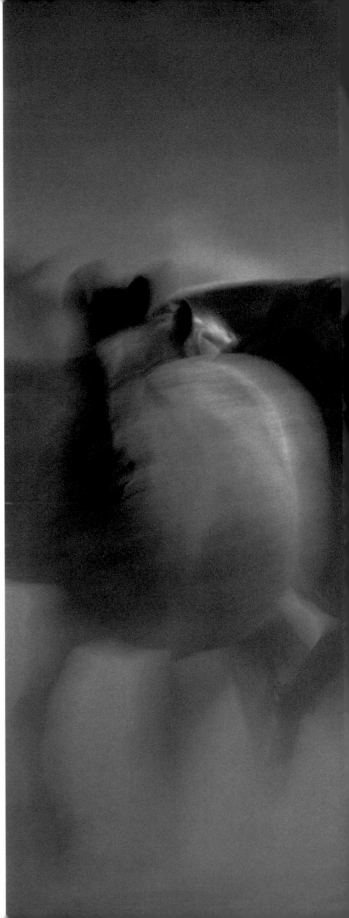

and every thing that moves upon the earth
after its kind. And God saw that it was good.

And God said, Let us make man in our image,
after our likeness; and let them have
dominion over the fish of the sea,
and over the birds of the air,

and over the cattle, and over all the earth,

and over every creeping thing

that moves upon the earth.

So God created man in his own image;

in the image of God he created him;

male and female he created them.

And God blessed them,

and God said unto them,

Be fruitful, and multiply,

and replenish the earth, and subdue it,

and have dominion over the fish of the sea,

and over the birds of the air, and over every

living thing that moves upon the earth.

And God said, Behold, I have given you every herb bearing seed which is upon the face of all the earth, and every tree in which is the fruit of a tree

yielding seed; to you it shall be for meat.

And to every beast of the earth,

and to every bird of the air, and to every thing

that creeps upon the earth in which is life,

I have given every green herb for meat.

And it was so.

And God saw every thing that he had made,

and behold, it was very good. And the evening

and the morning were the sixth day.

Thus the heavens and the earth were finished, and all the host of them.

And on the seventh day

God ended his work which he had made,

and he rested on the seventh day

from all his work which he had made.

And God blessed the seventh day,

and sanctified it,

because in it he had rested from all his work

which God created and made.

Praise the Lord, O my soul.
He makes the clouds his chariot and rides
on the wings of the wind.
He set the earth on its foundations;
it can never be moved.
He makes grass grow for cattle and
plants for man to cultivate—
bringing forth food from the earth.
How many are your works,
O Lord!
In wisdom you made them all;
the earth is full of your creatures.
May the glory of the Lord endure forever;
may the Lord rejoice in his works.

— F R O M   P S A L M   1 0 4